A Perspectives Flip Book

SCHOOL LUNCHES:

Healthy Choices vs. Crowd Pleasers

by Amanda Lanser

Content Consultant
Shahla Ray, PhD,
Department of Applied Health Science
School of Public Health, Indiana University

COMPASS POINT BOOKS
a capstone imprint

Compass Point Books are published by Capstone,
1710 Roe Crest Drive
North Mankato, Minnesota 56003
www.capstonepub.com

Editorial Credits
Jenna Gleisner, editor; Becky Daum and Craig Hinton, designers; Maggie Villaume,
production specialist; Catherine Neitge and Ashlee Suker, consulting editor
and designer

Photo Credits
Healthy Choices
iStockphoto: fstop123, 5; Newscom: Bill Clark/CQ Roll Call, 16; Shutterstock
Images: Basheera Designs, 13, GTS, cover, GWImages, 19, Lissandra Melo, 9,
Thaiview, 6, themorningglory, 26; Thinkstock: Mkucova, 22, Monkey Business
Images, 11, 25, Tetmc, 17; U.S. Department of Agriculture, 23

Crowd Pleasers
iStockphoto: Buzz Productions, 21; Newscom: Paul J. Richards/AFP/Getty Images,
7; Shutterstock Images: Markus Mainka, cover, Paul Orr, 28, Rob Wilson, 22, tacar,
17; Thinkstock: amanaimagesRF, 14, Digital Vision, 9, Jupiterimages, 13, Kelly
Cline, 19, Mike Watson Images, 5, senkaya, 25, travellinglight, 11

Library of Congress Cataloging-in-Publication Data
Cataloging-in-publication information is on file with the Library of Congress.
ISBN 978-0-7565-4993-0 (library binding)
ISBN 978-0-7565-5046-2 (ebook PDF)
ISBN 978-0-7565-5015-8 (paperback)

Printed in the United States of America in Stevens Point, Wisconsin.
092014   008479WZS15

TABLE OF CONTENTS

Chapter 1

YEARS OF SCHOOL LUNCHES

Students from Valley High School in Orange County, California, presented their meal to a panel of judges. The meal consisted of Kickin' Tacos, Zesta Fiesta Salad, and Yummy Tummy Bananas. The students waited as the judges evaluated their meal and the meals of other school teams from throughout the country. Each team was tasked with creating a healthy school lunch. It had to be appealing, tasty, and original. The Cooking Up Change cooking challenge asks high school chefs to create meals that are healthy and appetizing on the same budget schools use per meal. The challenge is meant to show that

Approximately 100,000 schools throughout the United States participate in the National School Lunch Program.

providing healthy school lunches can be tasty, creative, and affordable.

The U.S. government has provided students in public and private schools nutritious school lunches since the 1940s. The National School Lunch Program is one of the nation's more popular government programs. It has been the subject of debate and reform since it began in 1946. The public, the food industry, and politicians do not always agree on what a nutritious lunch is. They argue over what foods should and should not be allowed in school lunchrooms. They debate whether the government should even be involved in supplying lunches to students.

The argument over school lunches continues today. Those in favor of making school lunches healthier hope

more nutritious lunches will decrease overweight and obesity rates in children. The National School Lunch Program provides one-third to one-half of a student's calories in any given day. For that reason, supporters of healthier lunches believe the government should have an interest in making meals as nutritious as possible.

How the Lunch Program Works

The school lunch program is a federal program run by the United States Department of Agriculture (USDA). But each state government is responsible for administering its own programs. If school districts choose to participate in the program, they receive money from the government for the lunches they serve. Schools also receive foods from the USDA. When the program first started, these foods were distributed from surpluses farmers had. Today schools

Schools still receive some surplus foods from farms, now called bonus foods.

Look to the Past

The National School Lunch Program served three types of meals in 1946: Type A, Type B, and Type C. Type A lunches were intended to provide between one-third and one-half of the nutritional needs of a student 10 to 12 years old. Type B and C lunches were smaller. A typical Type A meal from the 1940s looked like this:

- ½ pint (237 milliliters) of whole milk
- 2 ounces (57 grams) of fresh or processed meat, cheese, or fish
- ¾ cup (170 g) of vegetables or fruits
- 2 teaspoons (10 g) of butter or margarine

receive foods such as vegetables, meat, dairy, rice, flour, and pasta from the USDA.

In return for the money and food from the government, schools must serve certain foods. Lunches must meet federal nutrition requirements outlined in the government-sponsored document, Dietary Guidelines for Americans. The guidelines recommend the amount of fruits, vegetables, protein, and whole grains students need. The National School Lunch Program provided 31 million children with school lunches meeting these requirements in 2012. It has served 224 billion lunches since 1946. Historian Susan Levine called the National School Lunch

Program the "single most important source of nutrition for children from low-income families." She acknowledges that without school lunches, many school-aged children in the United States would go hungry.

Room for Improvement

The school lunch program has a long history of feeding students according to federal nutrition guidelines. What foods fulfill those guidelines and how much food children need have been the subject of debate since the 1950s. Early critics were concerned the foods schools received from the USDA were too dependent on agricultural surpluses. This meant the types of foods schools received were inconsistent. This made it difficult for districts to plan meals. It also made it more difficult to ensure children received healthy, balanced lunches.

In the 1970s Congress allowed competitive food into school lunchrooms. That meant private companies, such as Coca-Cola and Pepsi, were able to compete with the school lunches served under the school lunch program. This decision has always been controversial. Since the 1970s some people have believed that children should not be able to choose unhealthy snacks at school. Many

Experts, school districts, and the public still debate the decision to have competitive foods in the school lunchroom.

Americans believed their tax money should support the national program so children received only healthy meals.

A panel of experts from the Institute of Medicine, which is affiliated with the National Academy of Sciences, proposed changes to school lunch nutritional standards in 2007. They recommended the program require schools to increase the amount of fruit, vegetables, whole grains, and low-fat and nonfat dairy in lunches. They also recommended schools reduce the amount of sugar, salt, saturated fat, and calories in each meal. In addition, the Institute of Medicine suggested that schools ban the sale of caffeinated drinks, chips, candy, and other snacks with low nutritional content. Panel participant Dr. Virginia Stallings explained why these changes were necessary. She said that because students receive a "significant proportion" of their daily calories at lunch, these calories should come from nutritious, healthy foods. "School campuses should be an overall healthy eating environment," she said.

New Rules

New nutritional guidelines for school lunches went into effect in 2012. These guidelines required increased amounts of fruits, vegetables, whole grains, and low- and nonfat milk in school lunches. Schools also had to decrease salt and saturated and trans fat in foods. Starting with the 2012–2013 school year, students throughout

the United States saw more healthy foods and much less high-fat meat and french fries in their school lunches.

Supporters of the new rules hope healthier lunches will reduce the number of overweight and obese children. In the past three decades, obesity has doubled in children and quadrupled in teenagers. Approximately 21 percent of 12- to 19-year-olds were obese in 2012. This figure jumped up from 5 percent in 1980. More than one-third of all children in the United States were overweight or obese in 2012. The new nutritional guidelines were aimed at reducing these numbers.

The National School Lunch Program cost taxpayers $11.6 billion in 2012. New nutritional guidelines help make sure that these dollars are providing healthy meals to students. The guidelines also help promote health and reduce national child overweight and obesity rates.

Students throughout the United States saw more leafy greens and fresh fruit on their plates in the 2012–2013 school year.

Chapter 2

KNOW YOUR LIMITS

What makes a meal healthy? This question has been the subject of debate throughout the history of the National School Lunch Program. Meals have transformed from calorie-rich lunches with full-fat milk, hot dogs, and pizza to meals of whole-wheat pasta, nonfat milk, and green beans. These changes may leave some students grumbling. Supporters, on the other hand, hope these changes will help students make healthier choices and maintain a healthy weight.

Creating a Healthy Lunch

The USDA released a new diagram to help Americans choose healthy eating options in June 2011. The MyPlate diagram includes an image of a plate and a glass. The plate is divided into four sections. The

The MyPlate diagram shows how a meal plate should look based on the Dietary Guidelines for Americans.

largest section is vegetables. It takes up more than one quarter of the plate. Grains are the next-largest section, followed by protein and fruits. The glass contains a serving of dairy, such as milk or yogurt. MyPlate replaced the 20-year-old food pyramid formerly used as a dietary guide.

MyPlate is an improvement compared to the older food pyramid guide and reflects new research in nutrition. But some experts have criticized the tool. They claim it does not address a few important points. The MyPlate guide does not make it clear that whole grains are better choices than refined grains. It also does not warn Americans to consume less soda, processed foods, solid fats, and sweets.

The MyPlate tool represents the dietary guidelines the USDA uses to determine what should be included on school trays. The 2012 school lunch guidelines called for double the servings of fruits and vegetables than previously required. At the same time, the serving sizes of protein and grains both shrank. The new guidelines also required one-half of all served grain foods to be whole-grain. Starting in the fall of 2014, all grain foods had to be whole-grain.

Controversy over Calorie Limits

The 2012 guidelines also created minimum and maximum calorie limits. Before 2012 school lunches only had a minimum calorie limit. Seventh to 12th graders had to be served a minimum of 825 calories at every lunch. The 2012 guidelines changed the minimum to 750 calories. The new

Meals Before and After

The new school lunch guidelines transformed calorie-rich meals to healthy, balanced meals.

A Typical Lunch before 2012
- Hot dog on a bun with ketchup
- Canned pears
- Raw celery and carrots with ranch dressing
- 8 ounces (237 mL) of low-fat chocolate milk

A Typical Lunch after 2012
- Whole-wheat spaghetti, meat sauce, and a whole-wheat roll
- Kiwi halves
- Green beans, broccoli, and cauliflower with low-fat ranch dip
- 8 ounces (237 mL) of low-fat milk

guidelines also added a maximum of 850 calories per lunch for high school students. They also included maximums of 700 calories for middle school students and 650 calories for elementary school students.

Supporters of the calorie limits use both history and food science to justify the limits. The National School Lunch Program was designed to provide approximately 30 to 50 percent of a student's daily calorie intake. Food science research shows that high school students require 1,800 to 2,400 calories per day. The new maximum is within the one-third to one-half guideline for students of high school age.

But the calorie limits on school lunches upset some people. Parents, lawmakers, and students were used to larger portions. Some students found the new lunches left them hungry just an hour or two after lunch. Other people believed students should be able to eat as much as they liked until they were full, regardless of the number of calories. The debate came to a head in September 2012. Republican Steve King of Iowa introduced the No Hungry Kids Act to the House of Representatives. His bill would have gotten rid of the calorie limits and other new nutritional standards. Supporters pointed out that before the limits were placed, students took only 787 calories' worth of food from lunch lines on average. This was well below the maximum. Kristi King, a registered

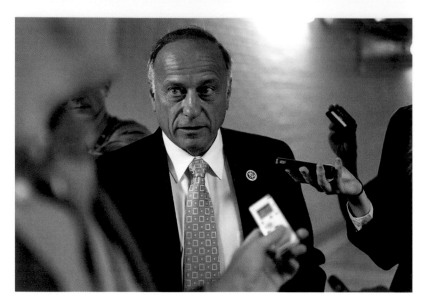

If passed into law, Steve King's No Hungry Kids Act would have eliminated calorie limits and new nutritional standards.

pediatric dietician at Texas Children's Hospital, said that if students were eating their entire healthy lunch, they should feel fuller, not hungrier. That is because the fiber in the fruits, vegetables, and whole grains takes a long time to pass through the digestive system. Margo Wootan, director of nutrition policy for the Center for Science in the Public Interest, said the calorie limits were good: "Not all students are linebackers, and [schools] shouldn't feed them like they are."

King's bill was never passed into law, but it did result in some changes to school lunches. Calorie limits are still a guideline, but the USDA will let schools decide whether to reduce protein and grain servings. This means students could see larger portions of meats and breads on their plates.

New Guidelines Making a Difference

Researchers at the Harvard School of Public Health were curious to see how the new guidelines affected the amount of fruits and vegetables students ate. They looked at the school lunch eating habits of 1,030 students in urban school districts in 2011 and 2012. They found that students took 23 percent more fruits after the guidelines went into effect in 2012. Vegetables were also more popular, with a 16.2 percent increase in consumption.

The 2014 project also studied food waste. Some critics claimed the new guidelines were causing more food to be thrown away. The researchers found that there was no increase in food waste after the guidelines went into effect. The study did find, however, that students continued to throw away the majority of their vegetable servings. The researchers concluded that schools should improve the quality and taste of vegetable dishes to get more students to eat them.

Studies found the new nutritional guidelines helped students choose healthier foods, such as fruits and vegetables.

COMPETITIVE FOODS DEBATE

Although the 2012 dietary guidelines required schools to serve healthier lunches, they did not affect what schools served at their snack bars or in their vending machines. Snack bars could still serve french fries, nachos, and candy. Vending machines continued to be stocked with competitive foods, such as chips, cheese puffs, and soda.

40 Years of Competitive Foods

A free-lunch program had just started when the USDA allowed competitive foods to be sold in schools. President Richard Nixon initiated the free-lunch

Schools are compensated for placing vending machines in their buildings.

program in the 1970s in an effort to reduce child hunger. In return for offering poor children reduced-price or free lunches, depending on their family's income, the government would reimburse schools at a higher rate for those lunches. But budget cuts forced the federal government to find other sources of funding school lunches.

Soon food companies were under contract with school districts to install vending machines in school buildings. School districts received athletic equipment and academic supplies from food companies in exchange for the vending machines. The companies began to market the junk food in the machines as healthy. They claimed the foods gave students energy and happiness. They claimed these

things were as important to a student's health as vitamins and minerals.

School officials and nutritionists believed competitive foods would change what students ate at lunch for the worse. At the time of the change, syndicated columnist Jack Anderson warned the change would allow food companies to increase profits "at the expense of children's eating habits."

Vending Machines in the 21st Century

Vending machine contracts can be worth millions of dollars to schools. Several districts and states have laws

limiting competitive foods in schools. But there is no federal law that does so.

Vending machines are found in fewer than one-half of all elementary schools, nearly three-quarters of middle schools, and nearly all high schools in the United States. Though common, competitive foods continue to cause arguments. One study looked at the effect vending machines and snack bar foods had on the eating habits of fifth graders. The study subjects did not have access to competitive foods in fourth grade. A year later they did. The study found that fifth grade students ate 33 percent less fruit and 42 percent less vegetables. They also drank 35 percent less milk than they did in fourth grade. In addition, the students ate 68 percent more fried vegetables, such as french fries. They drank 62 percent more sweet beverages and soft drinks. Experts believe that studies such as this reveal how influential competitive foods are on students' eating habits.

Making Competitive Foods Healthier

Competitive foods got a healthy face-lift in 2014, 42 years after they were allowed in schools. The Smart Snacks in School program was part of the Healthy Hunger-Free Kids Act of 2010. It requires school snack bars and vending machines to serve only healthy options.

The Smart Snacks in School program requires school snack bars to serve healthy options, such as granola bars.

According to Smart Snacks in School, healthy snacks are 200 calories or less. They have low amounts of sodium, fat, and sugar. Examples include granola bars, nuts, and bottled water. The snacks must also contain one of the following: a fruit or vegetable as the main ingredient; dairy, protein, or whole grain; or at least 10 percent of a student's daily requirement of certain nutrients, such as calcium, vitamin D, or fiber.

The 2014 school year brought dried fruit, 100-percent juice fruit juices, and whole-grain, low-fat, and low-salt crackers and chips to vending machines and snack bars. Low-fat and fat-free milk and yogurt are also available.

Agriculture Secretary Tom Vilsack explained his support of the changes: "Parents and schools work hard to give our youngsters the opportunity to grow up healthy and strong, and providing healthy options throughout school

cafeterias, vending machines, and snack bars will support their great efforts." First lady Michelle Obama proposed that regulations go one step further. Her proposal would ban companies from using their logos and names on the vending machines, lunchroom cups, and posters they provide to schools.

The USDA has found that making healthier foods available in vending machines and snack bars has a positive impact on student eating habits. It cites studies that show when students have more fruit and vegetable options in the competitive foods, they eat approximately 10 percent more fruits and vegetables.

First lady Michelle Obama (left), founder of Let's Move—a campaign working to end childhood obesity—wants to ban junk food advertising and branding in schools.

BEYOND HEALTHY LUNCHES

Supporters of healthy school lunches hope to improve students' eating habits. They also hope to reduce the number of overweight and obese students. But to do so, they may have to do more than limit calories and increase fruit and vegetable portions. Schools can encourage students to try to enjoy healthy lunches by improving nutrition education programs. They can also make sure that students are getting enough physical activity during the day.

Nutritional Education in the U.S.

A 2007 study evaluated 57 nutrition education programs throughout the United States. It found

Schools are working to improve nutrition education in an attempt to change students' bad perception of healthy foods.

that only four had been successful in changing students' eating habits. A 13-year-old student in Los Angeles, California, had one idea why nutrition education doesn't help students make healthier food choices. When asked if his nutrition class changed how he ate, he said, "Well, no. ... I think kids don't change because they've been eating it for so long they're accustomed to eating that way."

Dr. Tom Robinson of the Center for Healthy Weight at Lucile Packard Children's Hospital at Stanford University has ideas for improving nutrition education. He says schools should focus more on students' eating behaviors than on lessons about serving size and healthy food options. Classes should identify problematic eating habits, such as choosing junk and other unhealthy foods and

Salad bars provide more healthy choices for students, making it more likely for them to choose healthy options.

eating portions that are too large. Then they should focus on finding solutions for students. Robinson points to the success of hospital programs for overweight or obese students. These programs include family interaction, scheduled exercise, and specific nutrition education for each student's needs.

Things Schools Can Do Today

Changing school nutrition education programs takes time. But there are actions schools can take right now to help students learn about and enjoy healthy lunches. Action for Healthy Kids, a program of child nutrition groups, has studied ways to help kids make healthier eating choices. The group found students were more likely to eat healthy foods if they had a choice about what went on their plates. Action for Healthy Kids found in some cases that 25 to 35 percent of students used their school's salad bar.

Another way to give students choices is to include students in the decision making. Schools could include students in making decisions about what fruits and vegetables are served at lunch. Teachers could have students vote on foods. The principal could list the winners during the morning announcements.

Repeated taste tests and promotions of new, healthy foods also helped students choose healthier options. When rolling out a new vegetable dish, schools could run taste tests, games, giveaways, and contests to get students' attention. Action for Healthy Kids also found that pricing healthy foods lower than the junk food served in vending machines and snack bars increased student consumption of healthier foods. Making healthy foods more attractive by improving how they are served also helped.

Promoting Physical Activity

Daily physical activity is part of a healthy lifestyle. In addition to providing healthy lunches, schools should consider adding more activity to students' days. Only

What's on the Menu?

Salad bars can offer more than just lettuce, tomatoes, and carrots. Some schools are getting creative. Some days schools may turn their salad bar into a taco bar with taco meat, tortillas, lettuce, tomatoes, and shredded cheese. Other days students could create their own pasta salad dish. Baked potato bars are also fun and delicious. Students can dress their potatoes with shredded cheese, sour cream, kidney beans, or broccoli.

one-third of high school students get the amount of physical activity doctors recommend. Students ages 8 to 18 spend an average of 7.5 hours per day in front of a screen, be it a TV, computer, or cell phone. The result of these habits is that one in three students in the United States is overweight or obese.

Schools are realizing students need to be physically active throughout the day. In 2000 only two states and fewer than one-half of all school districts required recess. Six years later 11 percent of states required recess and 57 percent of districts required their elementary schools to hold recess. That year 79 percent of all elementary schools held recess. The Institute of Medicine claims that students who are physically active focus better. They also process information faster and perform better on standardized tests than students who are not active.

Healthy Lunches, Healthy Kids

To help students build healthy eating habits, schools can improve their nutrition education curriculum. Some experts argue that schools have a responsibility to offer only healthy food options to students. Studies have shown that having healthier options at school leads to students eating more fruits and vegetables. Changes to the dietary guidelines for school lunches will help schools plan healthy meals.

WHAT DO YOU THINK?

- How involved do you think federal and state governments should be in the regulation of school lunches? Give at least two reasons to support your answer using information from the text.

- Has your school implemented the new healthy eating guidelines, including calorie limits? If so, how has your school lunch changed?

- Imagine you are in charge of what goes into the vending machines at your school. What kinds of foods and beverages would you include and why?

- Pretend you are your school's principal. You have been asked to create a healthy habits program at your school. Come up with a plan for school lunches, nutrition education, and student exercises and activities.

INDEX

INDEX

WHAT DO YOU THINK?

- Do you believe the government should be involved in what students eat at school? Give at least two reasons to support your answer using information from the text.

- Imagine you are a student athlete. Would your school lunch give you enough energy for after-school practice? If it would, which foods give you the energy you need? If not, what would you change about your lunch to give you enough energy to get through the day?

- Vending machine contracts bring in a lot of money for schools, but they do not always offer the healthiest options. Write a two-paragraph letter to your principal arguing for or against keeping vending machines at your school. Include at least three reasons to support your opinion.

INTERNET SITES

Use FactHound to find Internet sites related to this book. All of the sites on FactHound have been researched by our staff.

Here's all you do:
Visit *www.facthound.com*
Type in this code: 9780756549930

GLOSSARY

carbohydrate—a substance found in foods such as bread and rice that provides energy

competitive food—food that competes with school lunches for student consumption

contract—a legal document that outlines an agreement between people or organizations

empty calorie—a calorie that does not offer nutrition in addition to energy

legislator—a person who makes or proposes laws for the state or federal government

processed food—food that goes through a complex manufacturing process and may have substances added to increase its flavor and nutrients and to preserve it

protein—a substance found in foods such as meat and dairy that is important to human health

reimbursed— money paid back that a person or organization spent

revenue—money made by an organization

surplus—leftover money or goods

PROS AND CONS: HEALTHY CHOICES

Pros

The National School Lunch Program feeds millions of students every day who may otherwise go hungry.

The federal government provides healthy meals, helping curb childhood obesity.

New nutritional guidelines have increased students' consumption of fruits and vegetables.

Schools can choose healthy options for vending machines and snack bars.

Schools can support healthy lunches with nutrition education and physical activity.

Cons

Smaller portion sizes are sometimes not enough to feed children.

The National School Lunch Program is expensive for schools and taxpayers.

In cutting out unhealthy foods in vending machines and snack bars or eliminating them altogether, schools lose a valuable source of funding.

PROS AND CONS: CROWD PLEASERS

Pros

The National School Lunch Program has not always acted in students' best interest.

Students are given a choice about what to eat, enhancing their decision-making skills.

Vending machines and snack bars are a valuable source of funding for schools.

Healthier lunches are too expensive.

Cons

The number of overweight or obese students is rising.

Competitive foods can negatively affect students' eating habits.

Because students receive a significant portion of their daily calories at lunch, the food should be nutritious.

Competitive foods are often large, unhealthy portions with high amounts of sugar and fat.

CRITICAL THINKING USING THE COMMON CORE

1. Consider both perspectives presented in this book. Do you believe schools should serve junk food? Or do you think schools should only provide healthy foods to students? Create an outline for a paragraph that explains your opinion. Include a topic sentence. In the body of your paragraph use at least three quotes from the text to support your opinion. (Key Ideas and Details)

2. On Healthy Choices pages 22–23, there is a quote from Agriculture Secretary Tom Vilsack. He said, "Parents and schools work hard to give our youngsters the opportunity to grow up healthy and strong, and providing healthy options throughout school cafeterias, vending machines, and snack bars will support their great efforts." On Crowd Pleasers page 16, there is a quote from Iowa Representative Steve King. He said the USDA's Vilsack wanted to "put every child on a diet." Vilsack supports the new nutrition guidelines, while King opposes them. In one paragraph, describe how their points of view influence how they describe the goals of the nutritional guidelines. (Craft and Structure)

3. Pick one side of the argument to use in a cluster diagram. In the center bubble, write the main idea of the argument. Add at least three other bubbles with examples of points that support the argument from the text. When you're done, explain why these examples support the side of the argument to a classmate or your teacher. (Integration of Knowledge and Ideas)

BOOKS IN THIS SERIES

SELECT BIBLIOGRAPHY

Doheny, Kathleen. "Does Junk Food in Schools Matter?" WebMD. 18 Jan. 2012. 4 April 2014. www.webmd.com/children/news/20120118/does-junk-food-schools-matter

Guthrie, Joanne, and Constance Newman. "Eating Better at School: Can New Policies Improve Children's Food Choices?" U.S. Department of Agriculture. 3 Sept. 2013. 15 Aug. 2014. http://www.ers.usda.gov/amber-waves/2013-september/eating-better-at-school-can-new-policies-improve-children's-food-choices.aspx#.U-4tidzyqG4

"National School Lunch Program Fact Sheet." U.S. Department of Agriculture. September 2013. 15 Aug. 2014. http://www.fns.usda.gov/sites/default/files/NSLPFactSheet.pdf

Piehl, Norah, ed. *Should Junk Food Be Sold in Schools?* Detroit: Greenhaven Press, 2011.

"School Lunch Calorie Maximums Protested by Students as House Republicans Introduce Bill to Repeal USDA Rules." Huffington Post. 18 Sept. 2012. 4 April 2014. http://www.huffingtonpost.com/2012/09/18/houserepublicans-introdu_n_1893936.html

Sifferlin, Alexandra. "Why Some Schools Are Saying 'No Thanks' to the School-Lunch Program." Time. 29 Aug. 2013. 15 Aug. 2014. http://healthland.time.com/2013/08/29/why-some-schools-are-saying-no-thanks-to-the-school-lunch-program/

FURTHER READING

Allman, Toney. *Food in Schools.* Chicago: Norwood House, 2014.

Etingoff, Kim. *Healthy Alternatives to Sweets & Snacks.* Philadelphia: Mason Crest, 2014.

Pollan, Michael. *The Omnivore's Dilemma: The Secrets Behind What You Eat, Young Readers Edition.* New York: Dial Books, 2009.

A Perspectives Flip Book

SCHOOL LUNCHES:

Healthy Choices VS.

Crowd Pleasers

by Amanda Lanser

Content Consultant
Shahla Ray, PhD,
Department of Applied Health Science
School of Public Health, Indiana University

COMPASS POINT BOOKS
a capstone imprint

ABOUT THE AUTHOR

Amanda Lanser is a freelance writer who lives in Minneapolis, Minnesota. She and her husband are animal lovers and have two cats, Quigley and Aveh, and a greyhound, Laila. Amanda enjoys writing books for kids of all ages.

SOURCE NOTES

Healthy Choices

Page 8, line 1: Susan Levine. *School Lunch Politics: The Surprising History of America's Favorite Welfare Program.* Princeton, N.J.: Princeton University Press, 2008, p. 2.

Page 10, line 17: Norah Piehl, ed. *Should Junk Food Be Sold In Schools?* Detroit: Greenhaven Press, 2011, p. 14.

Page 16, line 7: Nanci Hellmich. "Students Push Back on New School Lunches." 28 Sept. 2012. 6 April 2014. *USA Today.* http://usatoday30.usatoday.com/news/ nation/story/2012/09/28/kids-push-back-on-new-school-lunch/57842204/1

Page 20, line 7: *The Surprising History of America's Favorite Welfare Program,* p. 162.

Page 22, line 14: "Agriculture Secretary Vilsack Highlights New 'Smart Snacks in School' Standards Will Ensure School Vending Machines, Snack Bars Include Healthy Choices." 27 June 2013. 3 April 2014. U.S. Department of Agriculture. http://www.usda.gov/wps/portal/usda/usdahome?contentid=2013/06/0134.xml

Page 25, line 5: Martha Mendoza. "AP: Nutrition Education Ineffective." 4 July 2007. 4 April 2014. *USA Today.* http://usatoday30.usatoday.com/news/health/2007-07-04-fightingfat_N.htm

Crowd Pleasers

Page 4, line 1: "We Are Hungry." 15 Aug. 2014. YouTube. https://www.youtube.com/watch?v=2IB7NDUSBOo.

Page 6, line 4: Ron Nixon. "New Rules for School Meals Aim at Reducing Obesity." 25 Jan. 2012. 28 April 2014. *The New York Times.* http://www.nytimes.com/2012/01/26/us/ politics/new-school-lunch-rules-aimed-at-reducing-obesity.html

Page 14, line 8: Vivian Yee. "No Appetite for Good-for-You School Lunches." 5 Oct. 2012. 2 April 2014. *The New York Times.* http://www.nytimes.com/2012/10/06/ nyregion/healthierschool-lunches-face-student-rejection.html?pagewanted=all&_r=0

Page 14, line 10: "No Appetite for Good-for-You School Lunches."

Page 16, line 3: "Students Push Back on New School Lunches."

Page 16, line 15: Pete Kasperowicz. "GOP Bill Would Repeal Agriculture Dept. Calorie Caps on School Lunches." September 2012. 6 April 2014. The Hill. http:// thehill.com/blogs/floor-action/house/249849-rep-king-pushes-to-repeal-usdas-calorie-cap-atschool-lunch

Page 17, line 4: "We Are Hungry."

Page 21, line 1: "No Appetite for Good-for-You School Lunches."

TABLE OF CONTENTS

Shared Resources

YEARS OF CONTROVERSY

"Give me some seconds/I need to get some food today/My friends are at the corner store/Getting junk so they don't waste away." So goes the video parody "We Are Hungry" to the tune of fun.'s "We Are Young." It was put together in 2012 by a group of students at Wallace County High School in Sharon Springs, Kansas. The students were protesting the new dietary guidelines for the National School Lunch Program. The guidelines required schools to reduce foods containing protein and carbohydrates. They required increases of fruits, vegetables, and whole grains served at lunch. The guidelines also limited the number of calories each

The new dietary guidelines left many students who took part in after-school activities feeling tired and hungry.

lunch could contain. As a result many high schoolers, some of whom played sports or had farm chores to do after school, felt hungry by early afternoon.

Does Government Know Best?

First lady Michelle Obama sat down with a group of students at Parklawn Elementary School in Alexandria, Virginia, in early 2012. She and her lunch mates dug into turkey tacos, the lunch the school was serving that day. While Obama was visiting the school, she announced that new nutritional guidelines were going into effect in the next school year. All public and private schools in the nation that participated in the National School Lunch Program

would have to follow the guidelines. The guidelines would set calorie limits and double the vegetables and fruits served with each meal. They also would require dairy to be low fat or fat free. She said, "As parents, we try to prepare decent meals, limit how much junk food our kids eat, and ensure that they have a reasonable balanced diet. ... And when we are putting in all that effort, the last thing we want is for our hard work to be undone each day in the school cafeteria."

School lunches have been the subject of reform and new dietary requirements since the National School Lunch Program began in 1946. In the early years of the program the United States Department of Agriculture (USDA) created nutrition guidelines with an eye on the nation's agricultural surpluses. Students in public and private schools throughout the nation ate lunches determined by what farmers had grown too much of in recent months or years. By the 1970s the school lunch program had transformed into one of the country's most popular antipoverty programs. That is when President Richard Nixon declared that the program would supply a free lunch to every poor American child. The program was changed so that schools received money from the government for lunches it served to students. Schools were reimbursed more for lunches they served to low-income students.

Although vending machines helped schools earn money, they also introduced unhealthy options to students.

In the 1980s the program experienced budget reductions. In an effort to pay for meals, the USDA allowed private companies to take over some schools' lunch programs and snack bars. These companies were allowed to place vending machines in schools. The program now helps feed 31 million children in public and private schools throughout the United States. But some experts argue the National School Lunch Program serves the needs of politicians and private companies rather than the needs of hungry students.

School lunch chefs of the 1940s had to craft nutritious meals from a selection of agricultural surpluses that may or may not have worked well together. Today chefs have to work within a modest federal payment of $2.93 per free meal and the small income from lunch fees schools charge students to craft nutritious meals. Schools received 28 cents for full-price lunches, $2.53 for reduced-price lunches, and $2.93 for free lunches from the government in 2014. Some people believe nutrition has suffered in an attempt to meet these prices.

School lunch nutrition requirements were designed to reduce the number of underweight children in the United States in the 1940s. New nutrition requirements were enacted in 2012 to reduce rising childhood obesity rates. But reforming eating habits through school lunches does not address other important factors in childhood obesity. How much money a family makes and its access to fresh foods play as much of a role in a student's weight as school lunch program nutritional requirements.

School Junk Food's Role in Obesity

Most people agree that healthy food choices contribute to a healthy weight. They also agree poor food choices can contribute to being overweight or obese. But making healthy foods the only choice during school lunch may not help students obtain a healthy weight. A 2012 study

More than school lunches can contribute to overweight or obese students, such as a student's eating habits outside of school.

of 19,000 fifth- to ninth-grade students in 1,000 schools looked at whether selling junk food in schools increased the likelihood of students being overweight or obese. Researchers found no significant evidence that the sale of junk food at school increased the average weight of students. For fifth through ninth graders, having junk food available in school stores and vending machines did not lead to heavier students on average. But researchers conceded that junk food availability may lead to student

weight gain as students get older or have more control over what they purchase and how often they eat it.

The Right to Choose

Critics say the National School Lunch Program's new focus infringes on parents' right to decide what their children eat. It also assumes that the same nutritional standards are appropriate for students throughout the country, including those in cities, rural communities, and varied geographical locations.

School lunch nutrition requirements in the 1940s allowed for whole milk and rich foods high in calories. By the 1980s lack of funding led government leaders to propose counting ketchup as a vegetable. Faced with rising rates of child obesity, new nutrition requirements in 2012 called for nonfat or low-fat milk, more fruits and vegetables, and a limit of 850 calories for each school

Is Ketchup a Vegetable?

Secretary of Agriculture John R. Block was trying to think outside the box in 1981. He needed to save the federal government money in the National School Lunch Program. He proposed that the program count ketchup as a vegetable. That would mean that the ketchup on a student's hamburger could be considered a serving of vegetables. Ketchup is less expensive than a tomato, so having it count as a vegetable would save the government money when it reimbursed schools for lunches. Block's suggestion never became reality because many angry Americans protested the idea.

lunch. Critics argue the federal government has a poor track record of providing students with nutritious lunches. Some believe the choice of what students eat should rest with parents, children, and the local school district. They say fast-food meals, snacks, soda, and candy in schools should be available if parents, students, and the district believe their sale does not hurt students. They argue that parents—not the federal government—should be making decisions about what their children eat.

Americans opposed the proposition that ketchup be counted as a school lunch vegetable in 1981.

I'M HUNGRY!

School lunches now have less protein and carbohydrates and more fruits and vegetables. Guidelines also require new minimum and, for the first time ever, maximum calorie limits. The new requirements did not go over well with many students. Some students found that the healthier meals were leaving them hungry one or two hours after lunch.

How many calories a school lunch should provide has been the subject of debate since the start of the National School Lunch Program. Early on, experts argued about how many calories out of a student's recommended daily requirement lunches should provide. They decided that lunches should provide one-third to one-half of a student's total calories for the day. That meant lunches served to students in seventh through 12th grade were required to have at

In an attempt to avoid smaller school lunches, many U.S. students began bringing their own lunches to school.

least 825 calories before 2012. Starting with the 2012–2013 school year, lunches were required to provide high school students at least 750 calories but no more than 850 calories. Middle school students were capped at 700 calories per lunch. Elementary students couldn't be served more than 650 calories.

Students Protest New Lunches

Soon after the calorie limits went into effect, students all over the United States took notice. In a school district outside Pittsburgh, Pennsylvania, students were unimpressed with the new meals that replaced their

Some schools in New York City reported increased waste after the healthy meals made their debut.

lunchroom favorites. They began encouraging classmates to bring their own lunches from home. The packed lunches could include foods such as chips, candy, and soda. Soon the hashtag "brownbagginit" was trending on Twitter.

Students throughout New York City also took action against the healthier lunches. Middle school students dumped most of their vegetables into the garbage, describing them as "gross." At Automotive High School in Brooklyn, student Malik Barrows summed up why students were chucking healthy meals in the garbage: "Before there was no taste and no flavor. . . . Now there's no taste, no flavor, and it's healthy, which makes it taste even worse."

Perhaps the most public protest against the healthier lunches came from Sharon Springs, Kansas. A group of students and two teachers at Wallace County High School

produced a YouTube video. The video protested the new lunches. It quickly went viral when it was released in 2012, and it has been watched nearly 1.6 million times.

The group produced the video after they found that they and their classmates were hungry only a couple of hours after they ate the new school lunches. Teachers noticed that students were complaining of growling stomachs and became concerned that students were not being served enough food. Students particularly noticed the smaller meat portions. During the 2011–2012 school year, a meal might have included six chicken nuggets. The next school year, the same meal only included three nuggets. The size of meat cutlets also seemed to shrink.

The shrinking meals meant that students often arrived at after-school activities hungry. Student athletes found that they were not properly fueled for practice. Since Sharon Springs is a farming community, other students

Veggies in the Trash Can

The Harvard School of Public Health published a study in 2014. The study looked at whether the new dietary guidelines for lunches increased food waste in schools. It found that contrary to popular opinion, the new lunches did not produce more waste because students were throwing out healthy foods they did not like. But the study did reveal how many vegetables students discarded each day. Researchers found that 60 to 75 percent of all vegetables served and 40 percent of fruits were thrown in the trash. Although the new guidelines were not to blame for producing more waste, most vegetables were still not getting into students' bellies.

went straight home to farm chores. Student Callahan Grund explained how his lower-calorie lunch made his afternoon difficult: "I do chores before school and I have football practice after school and then chores after that, and I need a large healthy meal to help me get through the day." For many students at Wallace County High School, the new meals were not providing enough energy.

Legislators Take Notice

Soon after students began complaining about the healthier meals, state and federal legislators took action. Iowa Republican Steve King introduced a bill in the U.S. House of Representatives that would repeal the calorie limits and other new school lunch guidelines. His bill was called the No Hungry Kids Act. King believed that the new guidelines produced a "scant diet" many kids found was a "rude awakening." King claimed that because some children were overweight or obese, Agriculture Secretary Tom Vilsack wanted to "put every child on a diet." King went on to explain that "parents know that their kids deserve all of the healthy and nutritious food they want."

Lawmakers never passed King's bill. But his effort to change the calorie limits reflected how upset some Americans were about the new nutritional guidelines. In response to the outcry, the government kept the calorie limits but removed the requirement that schools serve

King's proposed bill brought more protein and carbohydrates back into school lunch menus.

less protein and carbohydrates at lunch. That was music to the ears of students at Wallace County High School. On the "We Are Hungry" YouTube page, the group announced, "Good news! The USDA will allow more meats and grains in school lunches following criticism of parents and lawmakers. To all supporters of our video, thank you for making your voices heard!"

LEARNING TO MAKE GOOD CHOICES

In the 1970s the USDA allowed private companies to sell foods in school districts throughout the country. Soon vending machines appeared in school lunchrooms. Schools began setting up à la carte snack bars where students could purchase food not required to follow the National School Lunch Program guidelines. Because these options offered students a choice other than a traditional school lunch, they were called competitive foods.

At the same time, some schools switched their entire lunch program to a combo meal model. Lunches started to resemble the convenient, easy-to-prepare food served at fast-food restaurants. The lunches

Combo meals of the 1970s were popular with students.

were often low in vegetables. The lettuce or pickle on a hamburger often counted as a vegetable serving. But the lunches still met the nutritional standards in place in the 1970s because essential nutrients were added to the foods. For example, french fries were fortified with vitamin A and iron to help schools meet the dietary requirements. A study of lunch participation in three New York high schools that switched to the combo meal model saw participation jump from less than 50 percent to 65 percent.

Junk Food Freedom

Selling junk food is big business for school districts in Texas. But some profits do not go to businesses. School groups, including sports teams and parent-teacher organizations, often sell junk food during school lunches to raise money for school programs. The fundraisers put school districts at risk of being fined by the state for violating its nutrition policy. In June 2013 lawmakers voted not to fine these types of fundraisers. This gave Texas high schools the freedom to serve junk food. But the state may run into problems with recently enacted guidelines for competitive foods.

Forty years later the Healthy and Hunger-Free Kids Act was passed. Once the new standards went into effect in 2012, some school lunchrooms experienced a similar drastic effect. Participation in their school lunch programs plummeted. Nimitz Middle School in Los Angeles, California, saw 600 fewer students eat school lunch. When lunchroom favorites were replaced with healthier options, students chose to buy food from vending machines and the school snack bar. At Mukwonago High School in Mukwonago, Wisconsin, there was a 70 percent drop in participation once the new standards were in place. Principal Shawn McNulty explained the cause for the drop:

"There is a reduction in nacho chips, there is a reduction in garlic bread, but there's actually an increase in fruits and vegetables. ... That's a tough sell for kids, and I would be grumbling, too, if I was 17 years old."

Learning to Choose

Some experts believe that selling competitive foods in schools has a negative impact on student health. They think that schools should offer students only healthy options to try to force them into healthy eating habits. But a 2012 study found that having competitive food

Advocates for competitive foods believe it's up to the students to choose what is right for them to eat.

available in schools did not increase the average weight of fifth to ninth graders.

In eliminating competitive foods from lunchrooms, schools miss an opportunity to help students develop good decision-making skills. With strong nutrition education programs, schools can help guide students toward healthier foods despite the temptation of competitive foods. Studies have shown that students need to be exposed to a vegetable 10 to 12 times before they will choose the vegetable on their own. Schools can sponsor taste tests, free samples, and lessons on how foods are grown and prepared to help build interest.

Schools can also improve the choices available in vending machines. North Community High School in Minneapolis, Minnesota, changed its vending machine pricing. Students paid 75 cents for a bottle of water and $1 for 100-percent juice fruit juices. But sodas and fruit drinks cost $1.25. By pricing the healthier options lower, the high school found that students drank less soda. In fact, water became the number-one seller. Though the school continued to sell sugary sodas and fruit drinks, students were encouraged to pick healthier options because of pricing.

Pricing soft drinks higher than bottled water or juice encourages students to choose healthier options.

HEALTHY LUNCHES, HIGHER COSTS

Most U.S. schools participate in the National School Lunch Program. Schools receive money from the USDA for the lunches they serve under the program. They get the most for the free lunches they offer eligible students. Each free lunch earns schools $2.93, plus another 6 cents for meeting nutritional standards.

When the new dietary guidelines went into effect in 2012, that money did not stretch as far as it had in the past. Fresh fruits and vegetables and whole-grain foods cost more to serve than traditional school lunches did. That meant schools had to provide healthier, costlier foods to students on the same

small budget. Larger districts that have more students on free and reduced-price lunch programs can meet the standards more easily than smaller ones because they receive more money, overall, from the USDA. Small districts with fewer students receiving free and reduced-price lunches have a harder time paying for the new, healthier meals without raising the price of lunch.

Many schools had to pay to hire companies to prepare and serve the healthy school lunches.

Schools Dropping Out

Schools were entering their second year under the new nutritional standards in the fall of 2013. Several hundred school districts had decided they could no longer afford to serve healthier meals. Some schools found that the only way to serve healthy meals was to bring in companies to prepare and serve the meals for them. By September 524 schools had dropped out of the National School Lunch Program because of cost. Another 3 percent of schools throughout the country were considering dropping out for the same reason.

More than 90 percent of U.S. schools reported facing at least one challenge in producing and serving the new healthy lunches in 2013. The increase in cost for fresh produce and whole grains without an increase in what the USDA paid schools for lunch made menu planning difficult. Other schools reported problems in improving lunchroom operations. Some schools had to purchase new kitchen equipment to cook food from scratch.

To make matters worse for schools, students were also not buying the healthy lunches. This further reduced the lunch money schools received. Voorheesville Central School District in upstate New York adopted the new nutritional standards for the 2012–2013 school year. It experienced a $30,000 drop in revenue from school lunches in the first quarter alone. Instead of buying lunch at school, students were bringing their own lunches from home or skipping lunch altogether.

Canceled Contracts, Canceled Revenue

Contracts with vending machine companies bring in a lot of money for school districts. Schools in the United States

What Does $2.93 Pay For?

Schools receive $2.93 for each free school lunch they serve. But not all of that money goes toward food. In fact, food only accounts for roughly $1.34.

Approximately $1.31 goes to paying the people involved in preparing and serving the food. The last 28 cents pays for supplies and other costs.

receive hundreds of millions of dollars from their vending machine contracts. In exchange for having branded vending machines with sodas, snacks, and candies in schools, districts receive a portion of the revenue from those machines plus other benefits. They may receive athletic equipment for sports teams. Other companies provide classroom tools such as posters.

When schools cancel the contracts in an attempt to reduce students' junk food consumption, they can face disastrous financial consequences. The city of Seattle, Washington, canceled its vending machine contract with Coca-Cola in 2004. In one year the district lost $340,000. Included in that total was $103,000 lost from vending machine sales and another $190,000 in a direct payment from Coca-Cola to the district. The money had supported athletics, clubs, and school events. Not only did canceling the contract cost money, it also did not improve student eating habits. Instead of purchasing school lunches, students went off-campus to purchase junk food at convenience stores.

The healthier nutritional guidelines put into place in 2012 put financial strain on school districts throughout the country. Schools struggled to pay for the healthier foods and new equipment to prepare and serve them. Other schools canceled vending machine contracts worth

Many students dislike the lack of taste and smaller portion sizes set in place by the USDA.

hundreds of thousands of dollars per year. Removing junk food from schools came at a steep cost to some districts.

Healthier Lunches Make for Unhappy Kids

The new dietary guidelines for school lunches are unpopular with many people in the United States. Students are unimpressed with the new meals, while schools find it challenging to provide the nutritious ingredients required by the guidelines on the modest income they receive from the government and student lunch fees. Others lost revenue when they got rid of the junk food in vending machines. One federal set of nutritional standards may not work for all schools in the country. More important, they may not succeed in bringing down childhood obesity rates, which is one of the main goals of the new standards.